Date: 10/7/21

J BIO WILLIAMSON
Smith, Elliott,
Zion Williamson /

Lerner SPORTS

SPORTS
ALL-ST★RS

ZION
WILLIAMSON

Elliott Smith

Lerner Publications ★ Minneapolis

To Denise, my No. 1 pick

Lerner Publications Company
An imprint of Lerner Publishing Group, Inc.
241 First Avenue North
Minneapolis, MN 55401 USA

For reading levels and more information, look up this title at www.lernerbooks.com.

Main body text set in Albany Std. Typeface provided by Agfa.

Editor: Shee Yang **Photo Editor:** Brianna Kaiser

Library of Congress Cataloging-in-Publication Data

Names: Smith, Elliott, 1976– author.
Title: Zion Williamson / Elliott Smith.
Description: Minneapolis, MN : Lerner Publications, 2021. | Series: Sports all-stars | Includes bibliographical references and index. | Audience: Ages 7–11 | Audience: Grades 2–3 | Summary: "A competitive recruit in college, Zion Williamson was drafted by the New Orleans Pelicans fresh out of his first year in college. Learn more about this exciting NBA rising star in this title!"— Provided by publisher.
Identifiers: LCCN 2020005959 (print) | LCCN 2020005960 (ebook) | ISBN 9781728414713 (library binding) | ISBN 9781728415000 (paperback) | ISBN 9781728415017 (ebook)
Subjects: LCSH: Williamson, Zion, 2000—Juvenile literature. | Basketball players—United States—Biography—Juvenile literature.
Classification: LCC GV884.W585 S65 2021 (print) | LCC GV884.W585 (ebook) | DDC 796.323092 [B]—dc23

LC record available at https://lccn.loc.gov/2020005959
LC ebook record available at https://lccn.loc.gov/2020005960

Manufactured in the United States of America
1-48652-49075-4/17/2020

CONTENTS

OVER

Williamson competes for the ball during the 2019 Men's Atlantic Coast Conference (ACC) tournament.

Zion Williamson was ready to play.
He wasn't nervous. After missing six games with an injury, standing on the basketball court felt great. His team, the Duke Blue Devils, had a big game in the 2019 **conference** tournament against the Syracuse Orange. Williamson was willing to do whatever it took to help his team win.

- **Date of birth:** July 6, 2000

- **Size:** 6 feet 6 (2 m); 285 pounds (129 kg)

- **Position:** power forward

- **League:** National Basketball Association (NBA)

- **Career highlights:** 2019 College Player of the Year; led Duke to ACC championship in his freshman year; No. 1 draft pick by New Orleans Pelicans; top-selling rookie jersey in NBA

Williamson took control of the game right away. He stole the ball and ran down the court all by himself. *Slam!* His dunk was the start of a great night. With his mix of size and speed, Williamson seemed unstoppable. Each time he walked on or off the court, he left the crowd roaring after him.

Williamson did not miss the entire contest. He made all 13 of his shots, a Blue Devils record. His 29 points and 14 **rebounds** helped Duke to an 84–72 victory. It was the freshman's best performance in a very exciting season. Williamson would help lead the Blue Devils to the National Collegiate Athletic Association (NCAA) tournament's Elite Eight, the national quarterfinals.

Williamson takes control of the ball at the start of a game against the Syracuse Orange in the 2019 ACC tournament.

Williamson was so impressive that he was named Player of the

Williamson and NBA Commissioner, Adam Silver, at the 2019 NBA Draft

Year by six different organizations. He averaged 22.6 points per game and 8.9 rebounds per game for the season. A few months later, the New Orleans Pelicans chose him as their No. 1 overall pick in the NBA Draft.

   "This season was a dream for me and the best year of my life," he said.

PATH TO GREATNESS

Believe it or not, Zion Williamson wasn't always the biggest player on the court. But he always wanted to play basketball. Growing up in South Carolina,

Williamson holds his mother's hand at the 2019 NBA Draft.

Zion often played point guard. His mother, Sharonda
Sampson, was his coach through middle school. He
says that she was "the hardest coach I had," but that she
taught him many important lessons.

Sixteen-year-old Zion completes a dunk during the 2016 Chik-fil-A Classic.

Before he started high school, Zion had a growth spurt. In eighth grade, he was 5 feet 9 (1.8 m). By the end of 10th grade, he was 6 feet 6 (2 m). Zion transformed from point guard to power forward almost overnight. Growing at such a fast pace caused his back and knees to hurt. But once his body settled into its new size, he became a better player.

"Once the pain went away," Williamson said, "I picked up all this newfound athleticism. I don't know where it came from. I just accepted it. Now, I had my ball handling and size, and the power forwards and small forwards who tried to guard me, I could fly by them."

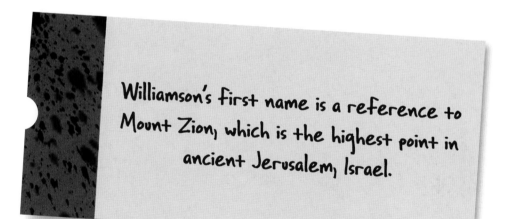

Williamson's first name is a reference to Mount Zion, which is the highest point in ancient Jerusalem, Israel.

Zion attended the Spartanburg Day School and quickly became an athletic star. He received his first college **scholarship** offer after his freshman year of high school. As he grew in skill and size, the crowds at his games grew as well. Zion was wowing everyone.

Zion puts on a performance for cameras and fans at the 2018 McDonald's All American dunk contest.

Zion and Coach Krzyzewski on the sidelines during the 2019 NCAA East Regional game

Spartanburg Day won the state championship three seasons in a row. Zion's dunks were going viral on social media. His name was trending across the country in the basketball world. By his junior year, he had 36 scholarship offers!

When it came to selecting a college, Zion had a tough decision. Some of the best basketball coaches in the country came to visit. His final schools included North Carolina, Clemson, and Kansas. But Zion decided to play for the Duke Blue Devils and legendary coach Mike Krzyzewski, known as Coach K.

Zion was the No. 3 **recruit** in the country. Both of the players ahead of him also signed with Duke. Basketball experts wondered if Williamson could stand out on such a competitive team.

In his first game as a Blue Devil, Williamson scored 28 points. He would continue to dominate college basketball. He became just the third freshman to make 500 points, 50 steals, and 50 blocks in a single season.

Zion attempts a shot against the Virginia Tech Hokies during the 2019 NCAA Men's Basketball Tournament.

Williamson
warms up
before a game.

All athletes make it a priority to avoid injuries. Williamson has learned why staying healthy is so important. At just 19 years old, he suffered two critical injuries. He had to work hard to get back on the court.

During his freshman season at Duke, just 36 seconds into a game against North Carolina, Williamson planted his foot when suddenly, his sneaker ripped apart. The sole of the shoe separated from the top, and Williamson's foot came out. He winced in pain, barely able to stand. Former President Barack Obama was among those cheering for Williamson as he limped off the court.

Williamson's shoe splits open during a game in his freshman year at Duke.

Williamson continued to cheer on his team from the sidelines while he took time to recover from his injury.

Williamson missed the next six games with a right knee **sprain**. Unfortunately, his next injury would be worse.

Williamson hurt his right knee in a preseason game for the Pelicans. At first, the team didn't think it was serious. But a few days later, Williamson had to have surgery. He missed three months of action.

During that time, Williamson spent hours every day working to heal his injury. The team's doctors and experts trained Williamson how to run and jump in ways that put less stress on his body, especially his knee. He learned landing techniques that could prevent injuries after big jumps. That's not easy when you weigh 280 pounds (127 kg)!

"It's not landing with straight legs," he said. "I can't let all my force go into my legs. It's a lot of technical stuff. I really couldn't explain it, to be honest."

Williamson takes a seat during a warm-up to give his knee a rest.

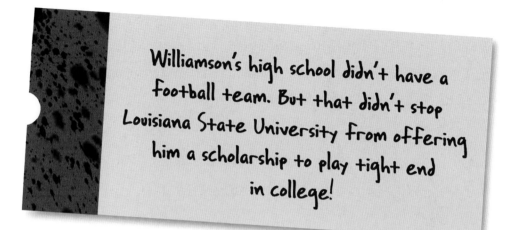

Williamson's high school didn't have a football team. But that didn't stop Louisiana State University from offering him a scholarship to play tight end in college!

Williamson practices with his teammates every day. He works on building his **stamina** by running. The team works on specific plays designed to help Williamson score. And Williamson lifts weights to help his body stay strong. The NBA season is long, tough, and extremely competitive. Players must be in great shape to succeed. Williamson is ready to prove he can be one of the NBA's best.

KID AT HEART

Williamson shoots
a few baskets
before a game.

Since the first NBA 2K game launched in 1999, the series has sold close to 100 million copies worldwide.

Williamson may be in the NBA, but he's not that far from his high school days. He still enjoys many of the same things he did growing up.

One of Williamson's favorite hobbies is playing video games. He is a big fan of the *NBA 2K* basketball games. Williamson was excited to see himself in the game. When he was asked to be the face of NBA 2K20 Mobile, he enthusiastically agreed.

Rapper J. Cole performs at the 2019 NBA All-Star Game.

Williamson is also a music fan, citing J. Cole and Drake as two of his favorite artists. Drake seemed to be a fan of Williamson as well. In 2017, the rapper posted a picture on Instagram where he wore one of Williamson's high school jerseys! Williamson has a large presence on social media. He has more than 4.6 million followers on Instagram.

Sneakers are a big deal in the NBA. Williamson made headlines when he agreed to an **endorsement** deal to wear Nike shoes from the Jordan Brand. Williamson plans to help design his own signature sneaker.

"I really can't express how happy and excited I am for this journey," he said.

Poetry in Motion

One of Williamson's hidden talents is his love of poetry. In high school, he took a creative writing class. He became interested in using poetry to express himself. Inspired by his teacher, Williamson started slowly. By the end of the semester, he was writing complex poetry.

"I wrote some real poems in that class," Williamson said. "At first, I was like, let me just get by. But one day, I was like, let me put something into this. I wrote a poem about the reality of the situation I'm in," Williamson said. "It's not so easy. I wrote a lot about that."

In high school, Williamson used poetry to help him deal with the pressures of being one of the top college recruits in the country.

Williamson smiles for photos at the 2019 NBA Draft.

After his first season at Duke, Williamson was the best player in college basketball. The New Orleans Pelicans were eager to take him with the top pick in the draft. And on June 20, 2019, the

Williamson during the 2019 NBA Summer League

Pelicans made it official. Williamson was No. 1. Blinking through tears, Williamson had a special message for his new fans. "Let's dance," he said.

Williamson started his pro career in the NBA Summer League. He was impressive right away, even among other incoming NBA rookies, mixing powerful dunks with smart passing. But his knee injury would force everyone to wait for his official NBA debut.

Williamson's return in January 2020 was celebrated like a holiday. A sellout crowd cheered as he was introduced in the starting lineup. After some initial nerves, Williamson showed off his star power. He finished his first NBA game with 22 points and seven rebounds. At one point in the fourth quarter, he scored 17 points in a row!

It was a great start to what looks to be a long career. Williamson's skills are well suited for the NBA. He owns a strong **crossover** dribble that helps him get past defenders. His footwork in the paint allows him to

Williamson makes a shot over DeMar DeRozan of the San Antonio Spurs on January 22, 2020.

Williamson warms up before a game against the
Cleveland Cavaliers on January 28, 2020.

score easy points by the basket. And his pure athletic
ability helps him block shots and run just as fast as
smaller players.

On March 13, 2020, two days after the suspension
of the 2019-2020 NBA season due to the coronavirus,
Williamson pledged to cover the salaries of all the
Smoothie King Center employees who would be out
of work. He said, "The people of New Orleans have
been incredibly welcoming and supportive since I
was drafted by the Pels last June, and some of the
most special people I have met are those who work at
Smoothie King Center. These are the folks who make our
games possible."

All-Star Stats

Williamson was the No. 1 pick in the 2019 NBA Draft at just 18. He joins an exclusive list of players who were selected first overall at a very young age.

Player	Age at Draft
Lebron James	18 years, 5 months
Dwight Howard	18 years, 6 months
Zion Williamson	18 years, 11 months
Magic Johnson	19
John Wall	19
Anthony Davis	19
Ben Simmons	19
Kyrie Irving	19
Karl-Anthony Towns	19

Glossary

conference: an association of sports teams that organizes matches for its members

crossover: a maneuver in which a player dribbles the ball quickly from one hand to the other

endorsement: a payment made to a player by a company whose product the player will promote

priority: something more urgent or important than other things

rebounds: the act of catching the ball after it bounces off the rim or backboard

recruit: a newcomer to a field or activity

scholarship: a sum of money granted to a student because of need or ability

sprain: an injury that results from the sudden or severe twisting of a joint with stretching or tearing of ligaments

stamina: the strength to handle a long effort

Source Notes

7 Duke Sports Information, "Zion Williamson Declares for 2019 NBA Draft," Duke University, April 15, 2019, https://goduke .com/news/2019/4/15/211799925.aspx.

9 "Zion Williamson on His Mom Coaching Him, 'Hardest Coach I Ever Had,'" YouTube video, 4:19, posted by ESPN, June 20, 2019, https://www.youtube.com/watch?v=OxbsVlWhXm4.

11 Langston Wertz Jr., "One of Nation's Top Basketball Recruits Resides in Spartanburg, Says Coach K Offered Scholarship," *Charlotte Observer*, November 5, 2016, https://www .charlotteobserver.com/sports/high-school/article112797658 .html.

18 "Zion Williamson Media Availability," New Orleans Pelicans, January 21, 2020, https://www.nba.com/pelicans/video/wsc /teams/new-orleans-pelicans-nba-all-star-rising-stars-zion -williamson-021420.

22 "Jordan Brand Adds Zion Williamson to Family," Nike, July 23, 2019, https://news.nike.com/news/zion-williamson-jordan -brand.

23 "Zion Williamson on Mom Coaching Him," YouTube video.

25 "Pelicans sign Zion Williamson," New Orleans Pelicans, July 1, 2019, https://www.nba.com/pelicans/pelicans-sign-zion -williamson.

27 Williamson, Zion (@zionwilliamson). 2020. "The people of New Orleans..." Instgram photo, March 13, 2020. https://www .instagram.com/p/B9sFV-nFTRG/.

Further Information

Conrad, Gil. *Zion Williamson: The Road to New Orleans.* Minneapolis: Full Tilt, 2020.

Ducksters: Basketball
https://www.ducksters.com/sports/basketball.php

Fishman, Jon M. *LeBron James.* Minneapolis: Lerner Publications, 2018.

Levit, Joe. *Basketball's G.O.A.T.: Michael Jordan, LeBron James, and More.* Minneapolis: Lerner Publications, 2020.

Williamson, Ryan. *Zion Williamson: Basketball Superstar.* Burnsville, MN: Press Box Books, 2020.

Zion Williamson NBA Page
https://www.nba.com/players/zion/williamson/1629627

Index

Photo Acknowledgments

Image credits: Streeter Lecka/Getty Images, pp. 4-5, 16, 17; William Howard/Icon Sportswire/Getty Images, p. 6; Sarah Stier/Getty Images, pp. 7, 9; Kevin C. Cox/Getty Images, pp. 8, 12; Tracy Glantz/The State/Tribune News Service/Getty Images, p. 10; Patrick Smith/Getty Images, pp. 13, 14; Sean Gardner/Getty Images, p. 15; Jason Miller/Getty Images, pp. 18, 27; Chris Graythen/Getty Images, pp. 20, 26; Karolis Kavolelis/Shutterstock.com, p. 21; Jeff Hahne/Getty Images, p. 22; Lance King/Getty Images, p. 23; Mike Coppola/Getty Images, p. 24; Michael Reaves/Getty Images, p. 25.

Cover: Sean Gardner/Getty Images.